Setting the Wire

A Memoir of Postpartum Psychosis

Sarah C. Townsend

For Jane,
With infinite
gratitude,
Sarah

THE
LETTERED
STREETS
press

Setting the Wire: A Memoir of Postpartum Psychosis
© 2019 by Sarah C. Townsend

Published by The Lettered Streets Press
Colleen O'Connor & Abigail Zimmer
Chicago, IL
www.letteredstreetspress.com

ISBN 13: 978-1-7335499-0-5

Cover design by Ryan Spooner
Interior design by Abigail Zimmer
Printed in the USA

The Lettered Streets Press aims to publish work we love & want to see in the world. We aim to work with writers who view publishing as a community. We aim to connect with readers who are moved & upended by words. We are a collective of sorts. We publish poetry & prose & what leans toward poetry & prose. We like blurring. We like projects. We support emerging voices.

Setting the Wire
A Memoir of Postpartum Psychosis

For Roger, Sophie, and Camille

I'll never leave you, I whisper as I nurse Sophie during the first evenings that follow her birth. I repeat the words like a lullaby, run my fingers along each of her cheeks and down her long legs still tucked in their fetal position. Now separate, we configure our bodies as one, her warm skin pressing against mine. She wears a white baby cap, my favorite, with pink lettering that reads, *La Jeune Fille*. Girl. She smells like buttered toast and French perfume.

I'll never leave you. I'll never leave you. I'll never leave you. I repeat these words with the rhythm of a birth contraction, like the ocean breaking along the shore. Sophie suckles late into the night until her lips slide open and the weight of her body gives way to sleep. But the repetition and reassurances can't stave off my departure. Altered brain chemistry pushes me outside of myself like a rip tide even as I fight to come closer to shore. I can't sleep. I'm leaving.

The first thing I must tell you is that with psychosis there is no *I*. Or rather, what it's like to waver in one's oneness such that in writing prose, it is actually more accurate to remove the pronoun altogether. A state of mind with no edges, a boundaryless territory where perception is a wild screaming cinema of thought, sound and image, each presenting its own degree of menace. Like wild monkeys, the shadows of fuchsia plants projected on a living room wall, a knife laid out on a bread board in preparation for lunch, a red flannel blanket stretched out over my husband Roger asleep on the couch, red checkered napkins on the dining room table, a blood bath, a warning, a siren from the street. ✦

Four fives and a four, four fives and a four, four fives and a four. Pacing the halls of the psychiatric ward at night, I bang my fists on the doors of other patient's rooms. I shout: *I need to go home! (I need to go home! I need to go home! I need to go home!)* As I round the corner of the nurses' station, a stocky male nurse blocks my path. A flock of orderlies descends. Thick forearms brace my body from behind and hands grasp each of my limbs lifting me from the ground. My back arches in resistance, and I scream as I'm hauled to a white padded room. Once inside, they set my body on a mattress at the center and bolt the door behind them. I leap up and press my face against the 12"x12" window, like a child on a car door, pounding my fists and wailing until I have no energy left and my body falls limp to the floor. I ache with a loneliness that transcends the fear of being alone, and then I release. I assume a fetal position and suck my thumb.

This will become a memory that I'm ashamed to remember. ✦

A single bead of water landing on the grate of a drain, a consistent staccato sound, *tuh, tuh, tuh,* the beat of a tongue flicking across the roof of a mouth. The air in the psychiatric ward's shower room is humid and thick.

I run my finger against the nipple of my left breast and peel yellow crust from its edge. I rub the coarse paste between my thumb and index finger and hold it to my nose. Recognizing the scent of sour breast milk, I scream out for my baby: *SOOO-FEEE!* My scream is guttural and reverberates against the tile. I'm startled by my own voice.

A young female nursing aid steps toward me in the shower stall and the rubber soles of her shoes suction against the floor. Her eyes widen and she leans her torso back as she aims a jet of warm water against my legs. I hover in the corner but she comes closer, cooing, *I'm only here to help you. You need to bathe. You need to bathe.* I dodge the pulsing stream. There's now a second nurse and I know that I'm outnumbered. *Get away from me!* I scream, insulted by their care.

They aim the water from two directions and it runs down my back and torso and along my groin and pelvis. *She hasn't showered since she got here,* one says to the other. My hands press against the jets of water and ripple against the pressure. I emit deep involuntary wails. I growl. One nurse tilts my head back and the other sends water cascading through my matted hair. And then I'm no longer there. I move into the not remembering, the silence, the space, the inarticulable.

From deep within, I emerge outside myself. I am an observer. The woman I see has not slept in five days. Her brain is loaded with medications, but they yield no rest. Her eyes are wild and her muscles tense. The nurses help her to stand and towel her dry. They dress her. She wears oversized red yoga pants from pregnancy, a nursing bra with snaps at the center to allow easy access to the nipples that have now gone dry, and a blue velvet shirt that is her mother's. When her arm grazes the tip of her ear, for a moment she is eight, nuzzling her mother's white cashmere sweater, numbing the pain of her parents' divorce. When her husband returns to the hospital to hold her at night, two bodies pressed together on a cold linoleum floor, she is an infant. But there is no baby here, only the one she has become, and the sweet one who appears in a car seat for visits. And there is no mother, only the one she longs to be and her own longed-for mother, now just a voice in the walls. ✦

When I wake from a nightmare recently, my blue ribbed camisole soaked in perspiration, the white cotton sheet beneath me now wet, I pull the fabric of my shirt up and over my head leaving it to drop in a wet ball. My moist torso, now exposed, is cold in the late night air. I seek comfort and want more sleep so I replace the garment with whatever top I can grab most easily from my dresser without turning on the lights and without putting on my glasses. I do this with the haste of a woman who is hunted yet without the benefit of full vision. In the bathroom, I sit on the toilet and then stare back through the door into our bedroom where Roger sleeps in a fog of sepia. I'm uncertain whether to lock the door or to prop it open. I cannot locate the source of danger. The thumbprint. The stain. ✦

At a beach on Great Lake Huron where I had spent summers with my father growing up, a friend from a neighboring camp asks me, *Was there something that caused your illness?* She asks this as we search for the raised patterns of fossils along the shore's gray limestone rocks. There is the sound of our water sandals rubbing against shale as her words disperse in the wind. I study the question, rummage my mind. What correlate? What antecedent? Was it something in the mineral vein of the rock? Some minor rupture resulting in a fault line? We stop to run our fingers along the spiral ridges of a petrified shell.

My brain had a seizure when the umbilical cord was cut. This I do say. *From that moment, I couldn't sleep. It was the onset of mania.* I speak with the flatness of a woman who cannot make full contact with the demon standing just behind the words, but also to provide reassurance to the concerned and academic eyes that face me and my perception that we have now, collectively, locked in on an explanation that suitably strips its meaning of any associated shame. I have momentarily anaesthetized the question. And yet I've underestimated my listener. She asks for more detail. *How many days did it last?*

Are we speaking in geologic time? ✦

I could treat her on an outpatient basis but we would need to meet every day. The psychiatrist says this to Roger and to a black leather couch upon which sits a new mother with lactating breasts. The world is infinite subtext and the waiting room a lineup of crazies.

The car ride: a fitful race along the I-5 corridor of downtown Seattle, gears shifting, pressure building. A father-in-law in the driver's seat, a burgundy Volvo 244, a mother-in-law seated beside him, a box to be opened along the way—a distraction? Roger riding in the backseat, our new daughter Sophie in the infant car seat at the center. They are outside the viewfinder, perhaps the silhouette of Roger against the passenger window. There is the matter of the return address on the package, a natural fibers company in Maine mistaken for a nuclear waste facility. The new mother is on the prowl for toxicity. She must protect her offspring from the dangers of the wild. *What!?* the mother-in-law in the front seat turns her head to the back seat and acknowledges exasperation. *Sarah, it's a present. It's from the Allens.* Two worlds slapping against each other. Crack. For a moment, there is entry. The new mother opens the package for the baby who is at this moment outside the frame. A slate blue knit cap, benign.

The new mother sniffs out madness in the waiting area of the psychiatrist whose office is in a neighboring wing to her OB/GYN's practice in a downtown Seattle medical facility. The room is a wash of white, clinical, peopled with the kind of patients who do not bathe. Those who stare off into space and apply makeup to lips and eyes that, while near the body part, are not lined up. This is how the waiting room appears to her anyway.

There is relief as she steps into an adjoining room so that she might nurse the baby. Ahh, a mothering function, aided by the closing of a door, the shrinking of the universe, contact with Sophie. Moist lips, the pressure of suckling. The mind: pulling, pulling, pulling.

Tugging, tugging. Back into the white space of the room. A nurse and a clipboard. The white noise of conversation. Shoulders against a wall. A name is called: *Sarah.* This will be the moment. The time has come for the woman whose shoulders rest against the wall to be whisked away, hospitalized, taken down a long white corridor, stolen from the father, the baby, the in-laws, removed. The terror of wanting what is needed.

But instead the outline of a man, C.W., MD, seated by a window with bookshelves behind him, he says, *I could treat her on an outpatient basis but we would need to meet every day.* The new mother sees his lips moving but there is no associated sound. She hears nothing after the prescription of an antipsychotic, which will allow her for the first time to sleep an entire day but precludes the possibility of breastfeeding. At home, sleep comes, heavy and drugged, a necessary syrup to stop the mind from ungluing. ✦

Fingers pressed against a wallet, the rushed opening of a zipper around its perimeter, chasing through cards assembled in the lining to find the business card of a therapist seen some years before during graduate training in psychotherapy at Northwestern. At home, in the room she shares with her husband, a call is made. *He wants me to take an antipsychotic!* she cries into the phone.

 I'd like to see you in a facility with other mothers, her former therapist tells her and Roger, her husband, who is on the line for support.

(At present, I can move no closer to this material. All I can say is that I was unwilling to sacrifice the breast.) ✦

When the on-call obstetrician cuts the tissue that connects Sophie to me, I am lying on a table in an operating room with bright lights. Roger and our new labor support doula, Diane, stand on either side of me. I feel their presence but cannot say for sure whether either touches my body. There had been talk of vacuum extraction as they wheeled me in a gurney from a birthing suite to the operating room and Roger and Diane hurried to put on surgical gowns and masks after first negotiating permission for a labor support professional to enter, a privilege typically limited to a single family member.

With little notice and a declining fetal heart rate, we had vacated the more sedate birthing suite with its view of downtown Seattle, wood floors, and pale yellow walls, the room where Roger had cradled me from behind, his arms stroking my belly, rocking me side to side. The hallways that I had paced up and down in the initial hours that followed the breaking of my water bag, at home in the bathtub, difficult to distinguish from the water in the tub. Women's ways of knowing.

Are they making you do that? one nurse asked, looking up from her paperwork as I walked slow laps along the hallway of the maternity ward. *She'll exhaust herself,* another nurse responded to the first.

I listened to a tape of our childbirth educator in my head. A cofounder of the doula movement in the United States and internationally, I call her *the mother of all doulas.* Doulas are childbirth and postpartum support professionals and, in my case, essential to survival. She will help me during the period of my illness. She will help me first and foremost simply by having mentioned in our childbirth class that she had experienced a psychotic break following the birth of her third child. This is not something that couples expecting a baby are prepared to hear and, like many other women, I dismissed this information as not relevant to me. Later, she would be the first to receive our call when I showed early signs of disorganization: inability to sleep, incessant talking, laughter followed by crying, the belief that I was having *really* good ideas.

Keep moving, our childbirth educator played in my head. *Walk during the early stages of childbirth.* I didn't want an injection of Pitocin, a hormone used to induce labor. Instead, Diane offered acupressure, gentle compression of my lower calf muscles and the soles of my feet, and then I walked the halls.

I know that my mother is dying because I can't otherwise explain why it is she tells me that she is unable to come to Seattle when I speak to her on the phone, or perhaps it is Roger who speaks to her. *We'd like you to come right away. The birth was more difficult than expected. Sarah is exhausted but cannot sleep. We need you to come sooner than we had asked.* She says to me, or perhaps to Roger, *I would like to come right away but I have an appointment scheduled through my HMO and the appointment was difficult to get. They need to review some recent testing in order to rule out cancer.* I actually have no idea whether she mentioned cancer. I know that my mother was unable to respond, that she had a doctor's appointment through her HMO that was difficult to schedule. I believe that she believed this was important. In my mind, she was dying of cancer. What other reason would keep a mother from responding when her daughter was falling apart? ✦

After seventeen hours of labor, I request an epidural. Roger and our doula Diane respond as agreed. They try to talk me down. *Perhaps you should wait a bit before making the decision,* Roger suggests. *We could try to move you off of your back again,* my doula says, approaching with her long massage-trained fingers. *I can't take the pain any longer,* I tell them. I am clear, and I can see in the subtle relaxation of their faces that my clarity relieves them. Back comes the German anaesthesiologist. I had dismissed him early on. *I won't be needing an epidural,* I had said confidently. I placed him in the category of Car Salesman. A fly on my arm. *Just so you know that I am here,* he responded, continuing on his rounds. ✦

In the moment when I request the needle for relief, I do not feel sold, nor that I have sold out. I have reached the limit, my edge. There is no one in the room who has walked farther down this path than I have. No one who yet knew to say, *If you want to turn a fetus, speak the anthropology of birth. Hold your body in the position of a woman who tends the field. Pick potatoes from the ground. Lean forward as you collect a pile in a basket. Feel your hands in the soil. Labor like your ancestors. Be in labor. Labor your labor. Work the field. Move organically.*

We try many positions, but on the whole we're inexperienced. ✦

I take the epidural, which includes several attempts to inject the needle into my lower spine, and there is a general numbing of the uterus that offers a period of respite. The labor and delivery nurse suggests that we sleep. Roger and Diane manage to do this after eating turkey sandwiches in the hallway. I can't bear the smell of food. I also can't sleep. I wait, on alert, awed by the force of nature. I am what the poet Sylvia Plath calls *a seed about to break.* ✦

Now Sophie is crowning. A nurse wheels in a mirror on a cart so that I might see the sweet lid of Sophie's head, her dark hair, for inspection and hope. Her head emerges shiny and wet only to retract again. ✦

There will come a time when you can no longer push. The obstetrician does not set an exact number. She does not seek to define the limit. What I know is that I've entered my third hour of pushing and that this is longer than many obstetricians will allow. This is something that I admire about her. She is merely setting the stage, an expectation, establishing a point of undoubted agreement. ✦

I can't feel my legs, I whisper to Roger. Then louder, *How can I push if I can't feel my legs?* He calls for a nurse and she turns down the continuous infusion of anesthetic through a catheter. A gradual reduction of numbness. A return of the rhythmic gripping. Pain: a compass. I latch myself to it. ✦

Medical necessity is what a doctor says when she's telling you that your opinion will be overridden, that her judgment prevails, that there will be no discussion, that you will submit and that in fact you have already submitted because the scissors are performing their scissoring function at the moment that the words exit her mouth. *Medical necessity,* the on-call OB calls out as she slices into my perineum. Sophie must be delivered quickly. ✦

We spread my father's ashes around the perimeter of a stone table and along the south side of the cedar log cabin he had inherited from his parents. The ashes, which turn out to be more like bone, we spread them. I do this with my father's partner Elizabeth in the fall of my junior year of college when we make the trip together back to Manitoulin Island in Lake Huron.

I save a small portion of my father's ash bone in an enameled heart-shaped box that sat on his bureau on the day that he died. Inside, there is a note in faded blue marker folded into a tiny square small enough to fit inside the box. It reads: *For a wonderful daddy on Valentine's Day.* I've added a heart at the top of the note on a sheet of paper torn from a small notebook. For emphasis, it would seem. I keep a second piece of bone in an egg-shaped box that has Peter Rabbit on its lid with his blue knit sweater and large inquisitive eyes. When Sophie was young, she would ask me to take down these small intriguing boxes and set them on the floor of the room where I had once been psychotic. Together, we'd open the containers and rub our fingers against the texture of the bone: grandfather. ✦

A dream. A close-up of my eyeball in a mirror. The shot is of an iris and a pupil looking back at what must be an eye. My right pointer finger enters the image and is pressing against the eyeball in the swerve of an S attempting to dislodge the fragment of eye, a gelatinous slice, fluid held together along the seam with translucent stitches. I consider upon reflection that someone—perhaps me— has taken a knife to the eye. A kind of gouging, but without apparent injury. Behind the sliver of eye, which I now hold between two fingers, remains an intact eyeball. The eye is intact and fragmented simultaneously. ✦

An earlier dream. A female figure in a black robe approaching on an otherwise empty conveyor belt. Her face is blank, a taut burlap cloth. I sense she is a mother, or perhaps the absence of one. ✦

When I lie on the couch of my therapist's office in downtown Seattle, a position I've assumed regularly over the past two years, I look out at neighboring buildings with the backdrop of open sky. I sacrifice my therapist's gaze, her eyes, in order to recline, but in return I enter another mind space that is not bound by words. One day I ask her to entertain the possibility of a narrative written without any overt reflection. *Why have lyrics when you already have music?* she asks. At times, in her office, I feel swaddled in a blanket of silence.

From my perch in my therapist's office, I imagine that I am Philippe Petit suspended on a tight rope between the former World Trade Center Towers. For several nights in a row, I watch the account of his stunning traverse in the documentary film, *Man on Wire*. Over and over, I replay the footage of his 1974 high-wire walk, awed by its beauty, its magnitude and impermanence. My response intensifies each time I remember that the structures he walks between no longer exist.

On a misty morning in August, Philippe approaches the wire, setting down one slippered foot and then the other. He holds a long balancing pole perpendicular to his torso and with each delicate movement he adjusts to the play of the wire, its sway and torque. Dressed in black, he is a silhouette against the sky, a dancer and self-proclaimed poet of landscape. In the film, now imprinted in my mind, the soundtrack plays a melancholy piano composition by Erik Satie. There is dissonance and harmony.

But what leaves me breathless, compelled to watch in perpetuity, is the moment in which Philippe lies down on the line, assuming Shavasana, Corpse Pose, his humanity collapsing into the sky. ✦

On my therapist's couch, suspended on the wire, I am one with the clouds. My mind is expansive; my thoughts, inarticulable, rest outside myself.

I think you are speaking about nascent creativity; something on the verge of words, form, feeling. ✦

As if there were the possibility of return, Philippe tests his footing. His face is still with concentration. But after only a short distance, no farther than the first cavalletti, his expression shifts like an abrupt change in the weather: his forehead softens, his mouth relaxes, his cheeks give way to a smile. There is a buoyancy of spirit signaling his confidence that the wire will carry him despite the many compromises to its rigging.

Philippe and a partner have spent much of the night hiding on a beam beneath a tarp on the 104th floor of the South Tower. For more than three hours, they have held their bodies still, hearing the footsteps of the night guard approaching and retreating, the lighting of his cigarette, the sizzle of the first inhalation, the crackling of his walkie-talkie. At 4 am, all is still and they break for the rooftop.

With a signal of recognition from Philippe, his friend, Jean Louis, posted on the North Tower, releases an arrow from a bow. His release uncoils a monofilament across the space between the buildings. When anchored, this strand will progress into rope and then cable.

The arrow lands precariously on the top corner of the South Tower, along its rim. Unable to see either the arrow or the filament, Philippe removes his clothing in the darkness and walks to the edge of the building. Listening to his body in the wind, he detects the movement of a thread on his bare thigh. The line. Later, Philippe will release too much cable and a portion of the wire will fall toward the ground. His partners will work furiously to reclaim the slack against the tension of the wind, and just before dawn, Jean Louis will announce through an intercom that he has set the wire. ✦

I'm setting the wire here with my therapist; I've lost her once before. There is no bridge connecting Seattle and Bainbridge Island, the mass of land where she practices and the one where I live. Only a ferry, and, when necessary, a telephone wire. When we first met ten years ago, I couldn't bear the cost of treatment. I couldn't tolerate the thought of myself as a line item. I questioned my value. Now that I'm ready to make the crossing, I realize that I can't do it alone. ✦

There is a remote risk of cord death, our golden-haired OB informs Roger and me, not intending to alarm us. *There is a small possibility that the umbilical cord could become dislodged from the placenta and result in a stillbirth.* She's matter of fact in reviewing the report. *Small possibility* does not register. *Stillbirth,* I hear.

A sonogram reveals that my placenta has grown in two lobes causing a *marginal insertion* of the umbilical cord at its perimeter.

A *marginal insertion* of the umbilical cord is also referred to as a *compromised attachment.* ✦

Cord death. Cord death. Cord death. My mind repeats this fear and so I sit still in a chair, my hands pressed against my hardened uterus, waiting for the movement that will temporarily ease my mind. It begins as a private conversation, Sophie's body somersaulting within mine, and then enters the public realm, her foot or elbow rippling against my belly like a pod of Orcas breaching. *La jeune fille!* Alive! The very movement that might cause her separation provides confirmation of her viability.

And on May 3, 1999, after twenty-six hours of labor, I bask in the beauty of her being. I worship at the altar of new life.

Only there *is* a cord death, just not the one we had been warned about. ✦

Alone in our bathtub, some two weeks after Sophie's birth, I soak my healing perineum in Epsom salt. My body feels the force of motion of a locomotive at high speed, my chest revved with adrenaline. I press my feet against the porcelain along the edge of the water, my palms firm against the bottom of the tub. I make every effort to throw on the brakes. ✦

Light reflecting on a small gold cross catches my attention as I sit with my mother-in-law in the living room of our Seattle bungalow in the middle of the night. The cross rests on her skin just above the neckline of her pajamas. She would be sleeping had I not come to her in the night. A mother seeking a mother. I'm afraid to be alone. At night. The cross pierces my gaze, the intensity of its flickering announcing itself as a significant object: a sign. *I'm having a religious experience,* I think to myself, and if I say it aloud, it's with the belief that I'm not actually disclosing this secret assessment. I exist several layers behind an exterior self in a mind that believes itself to be self-censoring. I believe that I'm having a religious awakening, a conversion of sorts, which I link most closely to Buddhism, and I know this by the way the moonlight spills into the bedroom beneath the closed shade. I know it specifically in the space between the bottom edge of the shade and the top of the windowsill. This is the place where God or Buddha or spirit is making an entrance. ✦

Mother-by-day, Dad-at-night, Mother-by-day, Dad-at-night. Words on a loop. I repeat these words as some obscure mantra in the first weeks after Sophie's birth. The transformation is marked by the removal of contact lenses and the putting on of glasses. My father wore horn-rimmed glasses. ✦

I sit on the toilet and place my hands against the floor. I fold forward from the toilet seat and press both palms against the coolness and solidity of the tile. I breathe. For a moment, I halt the train. ✦

My father's breathing was tight and sometimes labored. As a child, I saw it as my job to run cover, having conversation like bookends around fits of wheezing, never acknowledging the interruption in his speech as his chest convulsed in an effort to gain air accompanied by the tortured cry of an infant calling from the other side of a long tube. I knew to stay quiet by the way he clenched his jaw upon recovery.

He had a cleft in his chin, a Y-shaped fissure creating a subtle divide. When manic met his composed self, he dressed out of a Cole Porter song. He wore knee high socks, leather business shoes and long seersucker shorts. In the spirit of Dashiell Hammet's novel, *The Thin Man*, which he hoped to adapt for the stage, he drank Nick and Nora martinis and used a barber's blade when he shaved.

Originally from Sydney, Ohio, my father, Peter, admired all things Manhattan. Legs crossed leaning back in his parents' high back Victorian chair, he set about creasing *The New Yorker* at the fold and read aloud to me from the *Goings On About Town*. He delivered detailed descriptions of Broadway's current offerings, silent movies at the Met, lounge music at the Carlyle Hotel. Such delight we had in combing the menu. As the daughter of older parents and then the only child of a single father, my participation went without saying. We could make a morning of this activity.

At other times, a graying beard replaced his formerly close-shaven face and his body seemed heavy as if he could not lift his torso from the dining room table. He wore the pale pink shirt of a gentleman but had the hair and eyes of a madman. ✦

In the summer of 2015, I catch a glimpse of myself in the mirror of our master bathroom and for a moment, a swerve of time, I see my reflection as a witch. She has dilated pupils and a subtle curve of the left upper lip. A snarl. I startle at the witch in the mirror. What I feel is frightened and revolted, a combination of fear and disgust. I move quickly from the mirror and then look back to find myself, restored.

Later that afternoon, I look through a stack of photos I've pulled out from May of 1999, just after Sophie's birth. I recognize the small striped shirt with pearl buttons that we purchased to mark the one-week anniversary of her birth. I come upon a photo taken in the living room of our house in Seattle, a portrait of a family. Roger, his mother Shane, and Sophie are seated on our over-stuffed couch, the large porch windows behind them framed by the outstretched petals of pink and purple fuchsia, my mother's favorite flower. They are smiling. I sit below them, my back against the couch, included yet somehow set apart from this triptych. I've always been reluctant to look at myself in pictures from this period, instinctively skipping over myself in order to see my loved ones. But on this day, I zoom in, a close-up of my face, and I notice, as if for the first time, the intensity of my eyes, the subtle curve in my left lip, the corner of my eye tooth raised. They mark me as wild.

Later in the day, my younger daughter Camille, now eleven, passes through my bedroom, her hands feeling their way through the environment, and she picks up the stack of photographs from my bedside table. *Are these Sophie?* she asks. When she reaches the image from which I had recoiled, she says with compassion, *You must not have been having a very good day in this one, Mom.* She continues through the pile with tenderness. When Camille has left the room, I return to the photo, to the new mother's eyes, her curled lip. I stare back at her for a time and then I tear the photograph into small pieces. I want to destroy the record, as though it were not already documented at a cellular level. ✦

Four days before Sophie's twenty-six hour passage, I make an appointment with the Puget Sound Cord Blood Program. The date 4/29/99 is written in pen on my yellow copy of the *Patient's Authorization for Cord Blood Collection and Banking*. The consent form confirms my understanding that umbilical cord blood can be used in the treatment of leukemia. I learn that the blood from the often-discarded placenta and umbilical cord is rich in stem cells that support bone marrow transplant in the treatment of leukemic patients.

I speak to a young female research assistant in the gray light of a medical building. *My father died of leukemia*, I tell her, indicating the urgency of my desire to donate cord blood despite how long I have waited to make the appointment. What I do not tell her is my fear that the needle which draws my blood sample will give me AIDS and that I, in turn, will give AIDS to Sophie. I'm afraid that I will contaminate my offspring in the effort to heal a dead father from cancer. But with the force of childbirth approaching, I override that concern. I take the needle.

AIDS is not a risk of cord blood donation, but I believed it to be so. This is one way I know that my illness preceded her birth. A tremor. ✦

The catch is that I will need to hand-deliver my authorization for cord blood donation upon admission to the neighboring hospital where I will birth Sophie first in a hallway, then in a rocking chair, on a bed and in a bathtub, on the floor and on a gurney being rushed down the hallway after being warned of the possibility that one of Sophie's shoulders might get stuck against my pelvis.

I hand-deliver my authorization on a night when the nursing staff jokes that enough babies have been born to flood the kindergartens of Seattle. In the chaos of multiple births, including Sophie's, the document will not find its way into my patient file. ✦

On a recent morning, I close my eyes and see an image of my father with great clarity. I know it's a memory but the force of his presence is full-bodied, not at all like thinking *about* something and more like being there. For one thing, there is sound. He's seated at the grand piano in his rent-controlled apartment near Gramercy Park in Manhattan, pounding on the keys at the climax to Patti LaBelle's 1980 hit, "I Don't Go Shopping (for Love)." *And if you feeeeeel like I do-ooh,* he sings with his eyes closed, his head tilted back toward the ceiling, and then quietly brings it on home with a gentle touch of the keys and a soft voice, *I've saved it all up for you / So if you feel like I do / Well, we're long overdue.* He strikes the final chords and leans in toward the keyboard. Curtain. ✦

Listening to Erik Satie's *Gymnopedie No. 1* on the soundtrack to *Man on Wire*, I see myself standing before the Victorian pier glass that lived in the entry to our apartment on E. 63rd Street in Manhattan the year I turned eight. The mirror is framed in walnut with gold filigree and stretches vertically from floor to ceiling. Its top is crowned like a bishop's chair.

I'm wearing a pink leotard and tights and pink leather ballet slippers. My hair is pulled back into a short ponytail and my bangs march in a straight line across my forehead. My Scottish skin is pale; my cheeks and nose are flushed. I stand in first position, my neck long, both slippers pointed toward the outside edges of the mirror.

I study my face as the bassline chords begin. My light eyelashes. My hazel eyes. I let the chords repeat. They encourage me forward.

With the start of the melody, which I later learned Satie instructs to be played *lent et douleureux*, slow and painful, I lift my right arm over my head, my upper arm arching to the left, and rest my left hand on a phantom bar. I pause and imagine myself a member of the New York City Ballet Company. I point my right toe and reach my right leg out in front of me. *One, two, three. One, two, three.*

I stretch my leg to the right dragging the toe of my slipper along the floor, extend both arms out in line with my shoulders, reaching equally in opposite directions, set my heal down to standing and shift my weight: second position, *two, three. One, two, three.*

I reengage my right foot, point my toes, and send my right leg directly behind me, à tendu. In the same motion, I wave my right arm down, up and forward toward the mirror: arabesque à terre. The tips of my middle and index fingers make contact with the glass. I pause for the repetition of the chords, *two, three. One, two, three.*

I bring my right heel back in line with my left, stand tall, and rest my arms together at my sides, fingers reaching in toward each other. I breathe, *two, three.* I stare, *two, three.*

The *Ballet of Loss.* ✦

I exit my therapist's office on a Friday, following the painful routine where I sit up from the couch and anxiously pull on my Frye cowboy boots (purchased the year I turned forty) one at a time. Certain that I will be unable to perform this basic task successfully, especially because my right foot is bigger than my left and considering the thickness of my socks, with such close attention on me, the kind I experience as scrutiny despite her smile, that makes me wobble as I approach the handle of the door and close the door behind me—after all this, I hear Erik Satie playing in the waiting room. Alone, I have the impulse to dance in the open space between bookshelves and chairs and alongside a mirror: relevé, arabesque, plié, changement. I imagine dancing and then I imagine telling my therapist that I've imagined dancing because then I would be with her. Again. ✦

I've set aside a 1976 Polaroid photograph of me posing in my new school uniform for the Spence School for Girls. The photograph has cracked with age, creating a pattern of lines that appear more like the veins of a leaf than shattered glass. A cracked photo, framed in white. I'm wearing a plaid pinafore with a white collared shirt, a green wool blazer with the school emblem, loafers, and white ankle socks. I'm smiling, beaming actually, in front of the Victorian pier mirror that lived in the foyer of our apartment on E. 63rd street in Manhattan and in all of the previous and future households I would share with my father.

The reflection in the mirror creates what looks like two of me: a girl faced in two directions, one looking forward and the other behind. ✦

Our family of three sits together in the library of our 63rd Street apartment: a room filled with bookshelves, a leather reading chair, a large Oriental rug in oranges and blues, and eventually our dining room table. This is the room that anchors us; photographs line the desk and windowsill.

We're seated, three chairs pulled together. The air is starched and stiff. My mother's eyes are red and puffy around the edges. I can see that she's applied blue eye shadow but her mascara is smudged. I pull at the ribbons on my shirt. *Your father and I are getting a divorce*, my mother begins, clarity sending her forward. *We both love you very much*, she adds to soften the blow and then throws the second punch. *You and I will move back to Connecticut and Daddy will stay in the apartment for a while.*

My father's face tightens and he wipes the sweat from the rim of his glasses on his shirt.

I look at them, trying to take in the words. My father reaches out to me. I embrace him and then move just as quickly to hold onto my mother. Unable to sustain the tension, I walk along the perimeter of the room. I stop to pick up a photograph of my father and wrap it in a placemat from the table.

You don't need to pack anything right now, my mother says. *It's not happening tonight.*

Only it does. It happens right in that moment.

We go out for dinner at our neighborhood diner. None of us eats. I order fried chicken and mashed potatoes and drag the spoon around the plate, reconfiguring the potatoes into various shapes. My stomach aches. We hardly speak.

Later in the evening, my father sits in the living room reading and my mother lies on their bed and I walk back and forth along the hallway between the two rooms, returning to one as soon as I reach the other. I don't want to leave or to be left. ✦

Sleep is more important than eating, the dark-eyed obstetrician on duty informs me the morning after I give birth to Sophie when I tell him that I cannot sleep. While I seek relief, the obstetrician's statement only amplifies my anxiety. Then he prescribes Percocet. Percocet is for pain, and occasionally for laughter, but it does not help with sleep, I learned later, not for more than a few hours, and then only incidentally. ✦

Are you still taking that PERCOCET? my mother shrieks into the telephone from her Scottsdale desert home. I am, and it does make me funnier, but fear displaces laughter and I worry that that the medicine in my breast milk will harm Sophie, and that I will be culpable. Like most new mothers, I await confirmation of my badness, and so to avoid it, I wean myself, slicing the tablet into smaller and smaller pieces; little sleep gives way to no sleep.

Informed by stories of celebrities in *People* magazine, my mother fears my inevitable addiction. She reminds me, in a way she presumes to be helpful, that she personally refrains from taking any medications apart from aspirin. Ironically, my stepfather Joe once suffered internal bleeding by taking too many free sample aspirins from the physician's office where my mother worked as front office manager. She came home one day to find him lying in a pool of blood on their Mexican-tiled floor. Still, he had rallied and, with the passage of time, aspirin remained acceptable, optimal even.

Redirecting her support, I challenge my mother to a competition to see which of us can sleep more. Famously hardworking, she *requires little sleep* and enjoys competitive games like Pinochle and Bridge. I need her resolve. And so I challenge her to beat my record: four hours of sleep with Percocet. She humors me—I can tell by the concern in her voice—perhaps not sure how to interpret my invitation, as if she were concerned by the low bar. However much she sleeps though, amid her long-distance worry and the smell of desert honeysuckle, she definitely wins the contest. ✦

The view from on top of the handlebars of my dad's yellow Raleigh racing bike looks straight down Castle Hill Road. I press my gangling five-year-old legs against the u-shaped curve of the handles, lean my chest forward and grip the bar in each hand. My dad steadies the bike with his feet and we pause there for a moment at the crest of the hill, poised for flight. It's a quiet summer evening and the color of the sky, intensifying just before sunset, is a mid-1970s tangerine.

There's a subtle communication between us: his right foot lifting onto a pedal, the slight tipping of the bike toward the downward slant of the hill, my sweaty palms tightening against the tape of the handlebars and then, whoosh, with a push of his left foot against the pavement, we're off! We sail down the hill of the wooded Connecticut street, its intermittent suburban households with their white clapboard siding reduced to one stream of white light against a background of green foliage. I breathe in the smell of fresh cut grass and my hair whips across my face until the road eases into a set of gentle ripples. There is a soft clicking sound of our wheels coasting.

We turn into our driveway, past the maple tree that serves as my fort, and ride straight into the garage to the foot of the stairs that lead to the main level of our house. I hop off the handlebars onto the stairwell; my dad sets the bike against the wall and lowers the kickstand. *Well done!* he says, and we smile at each other for a moment. My mind bounces between exhilaration and relief.

Upstairs, we join my mother and my two older half siblings, Roberta and Ken, who are watching the *Sonny and Cher Show* in the living room. My father, standing with his hand resting against the upright piano, belts out the chorus of the show's ending theme song: *I got you babe, I got you babe.* I'm certain that he's singing to me. ✦

When Roger's mother Shane first arrives together with his stepfather Doug just after Sophie's birth, she brings out an old family photo album and sets it out on our dining room table. She walks us through its pages. *This woman,* she pauses at a woman in a gingham dress, *she was never the same again after childbirth. She never did come back.* ✦

During the weeks before my hospitalization on the psychiatric ward, I can only tolerate neutral material on television: game shows, cooking programs, and comedy. I particularly enjoy *LA Story*, the movie where Steve Martin plays Harris K. Telemacher, a disconsolate weatherman who finds the predictability of the weather in Southern California inherently unsatisfying. Eventually, *secret messages* from a freeway sign near his house lead Harris to unpredicted romance.

Even then, Roger tells me, I laugh at inappropriate times. ✦

Lying on the floor one week after Sophie's birth, I press my legs against the partition wall that separates our living and dining room. *I need some sense of boundaries*, I say out loud with Roger, his mother and stepfather nearby. This is my best attempt to articulate what is wrong with me. ✦

A few nights later, I'm alone in our bedroom—Roger, his mother and stepfather, his brother and his wife in the dining room below scrambling to organize my care. I've spent the afternoon drawing with pastels purchased from a neighborhood art store. I've drawn the outline of a shrunken girl with glasses. She is orange and running diagonally across her face is a shadow in dark blue. I imagine Roger and his family in the dining room below, a painter, a mathematician, an attorney and two architects conducting a charrette on this primitive work. I pull on a blue silk negligee from the top drawer of an antique dresser and snake my body along the floor, in part to listen although I can hear nothing but my own mind. ✦

I can't recall drawing the image of the orange woman with a dark blue section on the right side of her head. I notice that the glasses she wears are actually clear; it's just the right side of the woman's head that is darkened. The intuitive side. The sensing side of the brain. ✦

Pablo Picasso, Head of a Man, 1908
Blackened gaze evokes both blindness and introspection. Cast shadows on the face cover what were originally open, almond-shaped eyes.

Pablo Picasso, Composition with Violin, 1912
Incorporation of pasted paper is a reminder that this work is absolutely two-dimensional, yet the shadow on the right side of the newspaper has an illusory third dimension.

Henri Matisse, The Thousand and One Nights, 1950
When Matisse first composed this work on the wall of his studio, the elements were not yet organized with a sequence.

It's a kind of hell to have a notebook full of words that cannot contain a linear story and yet how boring it would be for you to read with any degree of linearity. The new mother, she couldn't sleep. She worried. She worried.

I'm exhausted from moving my pen on paper and I've hardly set down the words to explain. ✦

Which of these therapists would you like to see? Roger asks, handing me a referral sheet from my obstetrician's office, still believing that I might be capable of making this decision. He sits next to me in our bed where I hold Sophie. I reach out for the sheet of paper with one hand but the words have no meaning to me. Reading gives me a popping sensation in my head. I look back at him, confused. He talks me through our options and together we choose a nurse practitioner who specializes in postpartum mood disorders. I like the idea of having a therapist who also has prescriptive authority, someone who treats other mothers.

We meet in an office in a suburb north of Seattle where I spend an inordinate amount of time in the waiting area combing the patient consent form for devious content. Roger, an attorney, persuades me that the document is in good order and appropriate for me to sign. He puts his arm around my shoulder.

I don't think the antipsychotic is necessary, the nurse practitioner assures Roger and me in her office, where I feel temporarily grounded by some combination of proximity to Roger and sunlight through the window. *I wonder if the psychiatrist hasn't been unnecessarily aggressive. What you're experiencing is an anxious depression. It's not your fault and you will get better.* When she tells me that I can resume breastfeeding, I begin to cry.

We fill a prescription for an antidepressant and an anti-anxiety medication in a pharmacy in the lobby where I look at the pictures of an *Arizona Highways* magazine. I have the thought that there is a secret message for me hidden within those pages. I say something about it to Roger, who is distracted by more paperwork, and by now accustomed to my frequent use of metaphor. We spend the afternoon on the back deck of our house surrounded by deep purple iris and orange poppies. Sophie wears a wide brim checkered sun hat. A period of relative calm. ✦

In preparation for Sophie's birth, Roger and I cover the walls above her changing table with photographs of us as babies. This must have been at my instigation but the rationale is unclear to me now. A baby couldn't make out the images on the wall and what would it even mean to recognize a parent as an infant—a sweet black and white photo of Roger in a bathtub? I recall in puzzling out this arrangement on the walls that there was the immediate problem of fathers. Divorce and remarriage had resulted in multiple family constellations. The sticking point for me was the dads, how to represent them. The pain of lost fathers would be erased from this collage. Only babies and mothers and photos of a new father as a baby.

Eventually, drained by my illness, Roger requests more fathering. His father, Kim, and his stepfather, Doug, each make return visits to care for us. Something about this is so painful, both the privileging and the absence. ✦

Following Sophie's birth, I ask my mother to come alone. I'm afraid that my stepfather's presence will overwhelm me: his booming Bronx delivery. We'd spent years coaxing him to modulate his voice in quiet situations, when stealing a view of someone's outdoor wedding, a school performance. There is something about him that I want to remove from the equation.

My mother is honest in her response. She cannot come without him. *I rely on Joe to support me*, she tells me on the phone. My request betrays how primitive my need is. ✦

Roger, the nurse practitioner asks in a way that sounds like a trial attorney, *is it your intention to divorce Sarah?*

No, no it's not my intention to divorce Sarah, he responds. I must have been worried that he'd leave me. I remember feeling as if I were watching a scene of a play they had rehearsed. Or perhaps, my paranoid brain speaking, that I'd caught the nurse practitioner in her transparent efforts to challenge my paranoia.

She could not reach me. ✦

The nurse practitioner gives me a special notebook titled, *Postpartum Mood Journal*, which has black coil binding and pink pages. I wonder about the selection of the color. Blue is not an option, I suppose. No blue books for mothers whose hearts have been wrenched open, those who have been run over by a Mack truck, who have trouble exiting the hospital without the assistance of a wheelchair, and who spend the better part of an hour packing the few personal items brought on the day that the water has broken, including a cream colored blanket with a satin edge and a cotton sweater suit set out in anticipation of bringing Sophie home from the hospital. Blue is not an option for a new mother.

I actually like the journal. ✦

I begin writing in earnest on the pink pages of the *Postpartum Mood Journal* on May 25, 1999, three weeks after Sophie's birth. I've dated the first six journal entries 5/25/99, except for the second page where I've written 5/24/99, implying that I've gone back in time. 5/26/99 is written at the top of a blank seventh page and then crossed out.

On the following page, I've written: Monday, June 6. I have also written Sunday and crossed it out. I have also crossed out 6 and written 7 slightly above. June 7 is my mother's birthday.

The next page is also dated Monday, June 7. Monday, June 8 is written in black pen and 7 is written over 8 in red. These pages have been edited, corrected, or retrofitted to my mother's birthday.

With psychosis, I don't have even time to contain me. ✦

A few days after Sophie is born, I begin to wonder if my inability to sleep is a result of the epidural. I speculate that the multiple attempts to insert the needle into my spine has caused neurological dysfunction. I'm searching for an explanation as to why I can't sleep. ✦

On a sheet of notebook paper dated *5/25 or 5/26/99* (I'm increasingly unclear), just over three weeks after Sophie's birth, I've written: *Fear of sleeping is about not being with the baby.* ✦

Afraid I can't sleep with my mama baby or without her. ✦

When my mother and stepfather arrive, I'm on my third week with little sleep. While I ask my mother to lie down at my side when resting, my need for proximity to her in bed is excruciating. ✦

My mother and I spend the morning dressing and undressing Sophie in her new baby clothes. We begin with a dress belonging to my sister Roberta that my mother has brought with her from Scottsdale. It's made of faded blue chiffon and has three tiers with small, embroidered flowers. It's my sister's dress, but I also wore it as a baby.

I can't locate in memory how this activity came about, but I'm quite certain from my mother's expression in a photo of this day that whatever part of her thought it was a good idea to change the baby's clothes and then pose for a photograph holding Sophie in a Craftsman rocking chair is replaced by someone looking confused and uncomfortable, hesitant, as if she is going along with something against her better judgment. I must be trying to make something right with all the switching of the clothes: a white cotton dress, a Beatrix Potter cable knit onesie.

Later we get into a gray Chrysler that my mother and stepfather have rented at the airport. *So we'll just set the baby in the backseat,* my mother says struggling to place the infant car seat into its base. *Myrna, I've got the map,* my stepfather Joe bellows as he waves Roger's handwritten instructions over his head. His hand trembles as he puts the key into the ignition.

Seated in the front passenger seat, I open the glove compartment and file through the rental paperwork. I find references to Arizona: their street address, my stepfather's driver's license number—evidence that they are taking me home with them. *No Sar,* Joe says stopping the car for a moment, *we're not going to Arizona. We're going to see the nurse practitioner. Remember?*

Please, I say, *please take me to Arizona.*

During the car ride, I gnaw on a plan to overthrow the nurse practitioner by refusing the antidepressant she has prescribed in favor of homeopathy. I imagine taking small doses of whatever allergen is causing my unrest in order to develop a tolerance for the condition. I will ingest some herb or tincture that will prove more effective than the antidepressant and, by doing this, I will deliver Roger, who has returned to work at his law firm for the first time this very day, the opportunity to file a major lawsuit against the health care system. Something in me begins to erupt. ✦

I'm holding Sophie with my mother in the room when I tell the nurse practitioner in her office that I no longer want to take the antidepressant and will seek homeopathic care. The memory is a fit of actions: my pronouncement of this news, walking toward the office door with Sophie in my arms, the sudden scramble as I head toward the door, the nurse practitioner scribbling on a prescription pad with a pen, my mother standing, gathering up her black leather purse with one hand and clutching a brown paper sack in the other (my medication?), opening the door just far enough to stick my head out into the waiting room, making eye contact with a man holding a stack of files who I take to be a therapist, smiling in response because I want to pass as a colleague and not a patient, walking out the door of the office and past my stepfather who is seated in the waiting room reading the newspaper, walking down a flight of stairs into the lobby, sitting on a cushioned bench with Sophie, following the inhalation and exhalation of her breath, and then looking up to see the group standing above me in the mezzanine relieved, it seems to me at the time, that I have not left the building. There is general alarm. ✦

It has been explained to me that at some point during the course of these events, the nurse practitioner, now seeing the mania as flagrant, determines that my case is outside her practice area. She recommends to my mother and later to Roger on the phone that we seek care from a psychiatrist who treats bipolar disorder and psychosis. This happens on the Friday of Memorial Day weekend. We slip into a black hole. ✦

Out of options on a holiday weekend, we speed toward the entrance of Overlake Hospital on the Eastside of Seattle, sliding into the ER like a Big Wheel when you drag the brake. The world is electric; neon lights stream down the windshield and along the sides of our aging Volvo sedan. Roger drives and his older brother Haig, now a ballast, rides in the front passenger seat. I look past them out the front window and then over my left shoulder, my full attention on the light show and the forceful movement of the car.

Once inside, there is interminable waiting—the forms, the insurance paperwork. With my brain exploding bright lights like fireworks, I pace. I pace and I mutter. *You have to go slow to go fast, slow to go fast, slow to go fast.* After a period of time, we enter a beige-colored patient room with white fluorescent lights; an earnest young ER doctor arrives to perform an assessment. Roger is there to give the facts and because he loves me. He wears a powder blue shirt and his familiar Boston Red Sox cap, an allegiance to his childhood.

What is your name?

Do you know where you are?

Can you tell me what day it is?

Vaguely aware of the doctor's questions, I look out toward the hallway and see my mother rounding the corner. There she appears in a plumed white hat clashing cymbals, the grand marshal at the head of a parade. She lifts her knees up high, cocks her head back and marches forward with a smile. You can always count on Myrna to bring optimism and a stir of attention. Busy leading the band, she marches right past the door of the examining room and down the corridor. No one else seems to notice her. ✦

On the basis of this examination, I am voluntarily admitted to the Overlake Hospital psychiatric ward on Friday, May 29, 1999. I've been told this. It's a gap in my memory.

I move into the not remembering, the silence, the space, the inarticulable. ✦

My faculties sharpen for a period as I wait in a patient room of the hospital's South Unit psychiatric ward while Roger and his brother Haig cross the street to Larry's Market to buy me a toothbrush and toothpaste. I'm more concerned at not having my breast pump but Roger assures me that he will bring ours from home when he comes back to see me in the morning. I'm strangely comforted as I open the drawers of a faux wood dresser and then tour the adjoining bathroom with its robin's egg blue sink. There are two beds—standard hospital grade—but one remains empty. The room is sparse, mustard yellow, with linoleum flooring and the unit has the smell of cafeteria food and bleach. To me, it seems more like a low-end motel room than the snake pit I'd come to expect. ✦

Even with psychosis, there are moments of lucidity. ✦

In the morning, my mother comes to see the psychiatric ward and to assess the room. She has lobbied for me to have a single, afraid of any roommate I might have under the circumstances. Only later will they realize that I'm the roommate to be avoided. I will have my own room. Better yet, my own hall.

Roger brings her to see me together with his brother Haig. My plan is to depose them individually regarding my admission to the psychiatric ward. I want to compare their answers, see if I can detect any variation in the party line, catch someone vulnerable and off-script, find a way to go home.

Only I forget this part of my strategy, or lack the cognitive skill for making the arrangements, and so we stand in a circle instead, all together in the spare double room that is now mine. Still driving the questioning, I ask them in succession: *Why are you leaving me here?* Roger remains resolute, his soft face drained of energy like the last inch of water spiraling down a bathtub drain. *So you can get well*, he says. Following his lead, Haig and my mother repeat some version of these same words. For a moment, I accept their opinion and tuck it together with my own intuition—the thing that keeps slipping outside of my reach.

Then I ask to speak with my mother individually. I appeal to her maternal sensibility. *Why are you leaving me here?* I ask her.

I knew you'd blame me, she retorts, pivoting on her Cole Haan pumps. She throws the door open and shuts it behind her, exiting the room like a scorned lover from the scene of her betrayal. She couldn't watch me fall apart *and* hold herself together. We were both vulnerable.

Mental illness is hard to tolerate, no matter what side you're on. ✦

My mother can't stay, she tells Roger and the hospital psychiatrist. She has to return to her job. She will be back at a later date when she can make arrangements. This is what I am told.

I believe she is there just the same.

My mother remains present in this absent kind of way straight through the ten days I spend on the inpatient psychiatric ward. Though safe in the confines of her patio home with its Mexican-tiled floor, in my mind, she stays with me. I can hear her and my stepfather talking and singing in the walls of the hospital.

When faced with pain, my mother has always been resolute in her optimism. For her, there is no story that can't be rewritten. Like Blanche Dubois in *A Streetcar Named Desire*, she prefers magic to realism. We all seize whatever protection we can find from pain, even if it takes a whole parade of noise to numb our contact. ✦

Question written on a legal pad: *Are they here? I hear them crying.*
Nurse's response: <u>*Voices*</u>. ✦

She would stop during a visit, Roger's father has written in a personal essay about my illness, *hold up her hands—the fingers delicately poised, her head slightly cocked—look at you as if to say Stop! Do you hear that? What it was we were meant to hear she never said.*

Time after time she was convinced that her mother was in the next room. ✦

How many notebooks do I have to fill to say less? I started to write *feel less.* ✦

One function of this writing is the inoculation of feared memories: a kind of homeopathic remedy.

I tell you this now so I can let go of the fear. The fear and the shame. ✦

Walking me home from a play date in Manhattan one afternoon during the spring of my third-grade year, my mother says, *I saw Jackie O. in the elevator.* This name I recognize. *She was wearing my same coat.*

My mother always led with her glamour. That's how I see her now, in her double-breasted Jackie Onassis jacket and her bug-eyed brown sunglasses.

My mother's clothing is what I think of when I long for her presence. ✦

On a hot summer evening in 1977, all the lights go out in Manhattan. When you're eight, which I am, just having the hall light go out is cause for concern. This is the entire New York City skyline…all at once.

My father and I look out at the expanse of blackness from our fifteenth floor apartment. It's just the two of us: my father and I standing in the dark. A new reality. A new arrangement.

Together we climb down the muggy stairwell fifteen floors in the dark and come out into the air of the street, still sweating. On the way down, I grip the railing while my father talks about the electrical grid, but once on the street he says, *Let's run!* With that, he takes off down Lexington Avenue, arms stretched out like a bird, and I do my best to keep up, afraid of losing sight of him in the dark. I've often chased him, laughing as we run an urban obstacle course across benches and fountains and the planters that flank the entrances to apartment buildings, but on this night it's dark and I already feel alone.

My father comes to a stop when we reach an Avis Car Rental, a lone outpost with a generator. We stand in line with other New Yorkers suddenly interested in renting cars and emerge with the keys to a blue sedan. I stick close on my father's heels, still unclear about our plan.

I want you to meet my friend Elizabeth, my father suggests. *We can drive out to her house for the night.*

I don't ask him any questions as we drive along the FDR Drive toward Westchester County. Internally, I'm still keeping up.

Elizabeth greets us at the doorway of her house that sits on a wooded lot in Pound Ridge. She is a tall Yankee woman in her forties with short hair and glasses. She has the stylish appearance of Annie Hall. My father embraces her and kisses her on the cheek in a way that suggests familiarity. She laughs as he whispers into her ear. He introduces her as a colleague from his work at the Sun Chemical Corporation in New Jersey.

Sarah, I'm glaad to meet you. Your faa-thaar has told me so much about you.

We sit together in her dining room and she offers me a bowl of chocolate ice cream. While they speak about the blackout and the traffic coming out of Manhattan, I eat the dessert and then wipe the sides of the white Bennington bowl with a paper napkin.

I am planning to wash that bowl, Elizabeth assures me. I hesitate and then continue on, wiping away any evidence of pleasure in her offering.

That night they sleep together in her master bedroom and I sleep in an antique sleigh bed in a guest room that smells of mothballs. Underneath the sheets, I cocoon myself in a green crocheted blanket and hold the sides closed. It's a web of skin meant to hold me through the night. ✦

Skin (n.)

1. The membranous tissue forming the external covering or integument of an animal and consisting in vertebrates of the epidermis and dermis.
2. A usually thin, closely adhering outer layer: the skin of a peach; a sausage skin; the skin of an aircraft.
3. *Informal* One's life or physical survival.

American Heritage Dictionary

At some point, over time, perhaps intermittently, I came to believe I was damaged. ✦

I have written to the edge of my ambivalence. ✦

It turns out that fascia, the web of connective tissues that hold our bodies together, begin developing in utero. This integrating mesh that envelops our bones, muscles, and organs reflects the sensory perception of the womb and early infancy. I think this is why I take refuge in hot baths with eucalyptus oil, the desert sun, or a heated yoga studio. A finger set between the eyebrows and above the long bone of the nose. *The third eye*, I've heard it called.

Our fascia recall positions of anxiety long after the trigger has passed. Memory is written into the body.

The prolonged postures associated with yin yoga tear the fascia in a manner that allows for new growth. Sustained tension leads to integration.

I'm interested in the idea that something torn apart can be more healthfully reconstructed. ✦

Straddling the wire between his legs, Philippe does the unthinkable: he looks down. In his mind, he sees the crowd. He hears their murmur. ✦

At my one-year follow-up appointment, my OB is on maternity leave. A young male colleague with glasses and a white lab coat pops his head into the examining room where I wait in a paper gown. *I'll be with you in just a minute,* he promises, smiling, and then heads back out the door. When he returns, I catch sight of a notepad he carries with the word *attachment* written in black ink. I feel a jolt as my eyes trace the letters. I breathe in shame. I assume this note is a reminder to assess my attachment to Sophie. A therapist myself, I recognize the importance of observing the emotional connection between a mother and her baby following a postpartum mood disorder, but I'm shocked by the word and its being directed at me. Not that he ever says it out loud.

I tell him about Sophie's upcoming birthday party, the large number of guests, the eight quiches that I've made from scratch, the little blueberry pie she will eat. . . .

If there is a physical examination, I don't remember it. ✦

When I first begin seeing my therapist in 2003, four years after Sophie's birth, I risk the topic of attachment. Since the time of my illness, many caregivers have assured me that there has been no negative impact on Sophie. They have testified to her resiliency, Roger's consistent presence, and the many loving arms that held her in my absence. During the time of my hospitalization, the psychiatrist assured Roger that bringing her to see me every other day was *certainly sufficient.*

This is not the answer that my therapist gives. *We don't know the impact,* she acknowledges, her words both stinging and accurate. *We'll just have to wait and see. But to say there is no impact . . . that seriously underestimates the significance of a mother, don't you think?* ✦

It's the formaldehyde, my father says, rubbing the plastic on the seat of his car one afternoon in the driveway of his partner Elizabeth's house. He had worked for a chemical corporation. He was dying of leukemia. This word rattles in my head more than ten years later as I lie on the floor with my mother-in-law outside my bedroom where Sophie sleeps in her bassinet and Roger sleeps in our bed. It's the middle of the night, two weeks after Sophie's birth, and we lie there with our legs up the wall, breathing but still not sleeping. *What's happening to me?* I ask her. *It's the hormones,* she repeats.

On the day my father dies, I stand over his bed at Columbia Presbyterian Hospital in New York City together with Elizabeth, shocked by the utter transformation of his body. He lies flat beneath me, his skin so inflated that he no longer resembles a person. He looks more like a mass of undifferentiated flesh, but I sense that he has waited for me.

Keep talking to him, Elizabeth pleads, hoping to maintain his consciousness. I tell him that I love him and then I don't know what to say, so I recount my trip on the train from my college in Connecticut and the subway from Grand Central Station to 168th street. At some point, I stop talking and walk out to a pay phone down the hall to call my mother in Scottsdale. *Dad's dying,* I tell her. It seems fitting to include her. I return to find Elizabeth walking in the hall. I hear the word code as hospital staff scramble toward his room and someone calls for his doctor. *Is he dead?* Elizabeth asks the nurse and, in a moment of grace, she whispers, *Yes.*

That night, suddenly thrown together, Elizabeth and I drive to her house in Pound Ridge. She makes a bed for herself on the couch and directs me to the master bedroom that she has shared with my father. I run my hand across the wooden container on the dresser which holds his cuff links and the heart-shaped box that I had given him on Valentine's Day when I was twelve, the year I moved to Arizona with my mother and stepfather. I'm afraid to sleep in the room, haunted both by his presence and his absence.

In the early morning, I walk out to the living room to find Elizabeth awake on the couch, weeping, and though we have never before had physical intimacy, I fold my nineteen-year-old body against hers, desperate to be held. ✦

I find that books provide a certain inherent containment, what with the binding and the cover. When Sophie was a toddler, she would place her foot along the inside fold of whatever book I was reading to her (*Make Way for Ducklings, Blueberries for Sal, Barnyard Dance*), her warm body pressed into my lap. She seemed intent on entering the story physically. Joining the world in those pages.

For me, each book testifies that another human being has made it from beginning to end. ✦

According to the psychoanalyst Esther Bick, our first psychological need is to be held together physically and in the mind of the parent.

Through an accumulated experience of holding, the infant develops the sense of an external boundary sometimes referred to as *psychic skin*. ✦

Bick's ideas developed alongside the psychoanalyst Wilfred Bion's "A Theory of Thinking" and in the context of the body of work presented by the psychoanalyst Melanie Klein.

There can be a sense of falling apart in the mother stirred by the newborn baby: a container in need of containment.

At times, the baby's presence can be experienced as *a threat to the mother's sense of her own mind and identity*.

Frances Tustin, a student of Esther Bick, remarked that psychosis is so shocking because extreme states of mind in the infant are typically expressed within the privacy of parental sheltering. ✦

When I am five or six and we live in our house by the pond in Connecticut in what I consider to be my childhood home (although my family would only live there until I had completed the first grade), my parents move their bedroom down to a finished basement. This rearrangement coincides with my middle brother Ken's return to Minneapolis, his childhood home. I register the loss in connection with no longer being able to ride my tricycle around the pool table. I like to ride its perimeter, stopping to toss billiard balls onto the table and then riding to each corner to collect the balls and distribute them again. I like to race between the pockets, hear the clinking of the porcelain.

The replacement of the pool table with my parents' bedroom means that we are now separated by a full flight of stairs and a dank and terror-inducing garage that must be crossed in order to reach their bedroom.

On more than one occasion, I wake in the night to find that my door has been closed and the hall light, no longer needed, turned off for the evening. In a panic, I run toward the door, tripping over furniture or toys, a small red rocking chair, a doll-size brass bed, reaching my hand out in the dark to find the door handle and presumably the hallway, the stairs, the gauntlet. I can't remember the passage, only the obstacles and groping for the door. ✦

Ventura, California: Sophie is three. We're staying on a street that runs perpendicular to the beach with three male friends of Roger's from high school in a house that is *six from the sand*. Sophie is dressed for the French Riviera: a light blue bathing suit with a ruffle at the bottom, a wide brim hat and sunglasses. The beach smells of salt, suntan lotion, and In-N-Out Burger. The now thirty-something high school boys play Smash Ball and body surf while Sophie and I park ourselves on towels just below the dunes. For several days in a row, I have championed the merits of building a castle in wet sand but Sophie won't budge. I argue against the inefficiency of our method: the endless trips to fill her red plastic pitcher and buckets with water, their minimal impact on the dry sand that surrounds our towels. She settles into the squat of a sumo wrestler and then I hold her in my lap. *The water won't come up there*, I assure her, pointing to a section of beach just below the high water mark. The tide is heading out.

How do you think it got wet then? she asks, her resistance finally clear to me. She is uncertain when and how fast the water might return.

You cannot command memory. The mind has its own pace. ✦

Like Philippe approaching the high wire, I have one foot anchored on the building, one foot anchored on the wire. ✦

For a long time, my greatest fear was that I would forget my postpartum illness, and in a way I do, as I have to work hard to get back in there close. But when you hold yourself still, seated in a forward fold, and breathe deep within your side body, well . . . you feel something. ✦

Even in the height of my disturbance, I manage to remember our home phone number. I run out to the phone booth in the hall of the psychiatric ward to call Roger. Sometimes at odd hours of the night.

At other times, the staff does the calling. Roger is the only one who can relax me. ✦

On occasion, it occurs to me that I am hospitalized on a voluntary basis, and so I approach the nurse's station to request to sign myself out. A nurse with red hair and a sturdy personality—a perpetual advocate—gets Roger on the phone so that he might remind me that it is in my best interest to stay put. That's how much I trust him. Enough to agree to stay in a psychiatric facility. Without my baby. ✦

At home, in our backyard: black-eyed Susans, anemone japonica, alpine strawberries, violet lupin, the memory of fragrant lilacs once heavy on the branch. ✦

There is no language to encapsulate the love that Roger offers to me and to Sophie during the time that I am separate from them. In the evenings, he drives across the 520 bridge from Seattle to Bellevue, Washington, to lie down with me on the floor of the Quiet Room, our faces pressed against linoleum. It was as if I needed to wear him, only I was not the only baby. Sometimes he made two trips in a day. One trip to bring Sophie to see me. ✦

Because of her agitation, she was placed in locked seclusion and she had a sitter with her twenty-four hours per day.

While *sitter* might sound derogatory, or suggest that the function of this role is solely to prevent harm to self or others, in assigning me one the hospital creates a necessary holding environment.

When I read an academic paper that describes the use of music as a maternal container in the treatment of psychosis, I begin to wonder about this possibility.

Erik Satie's *Gymnopedie No. 1*, the music on the soundtrack to *Man On Wire*, is an alternating progression of two major seventh chords. A kind of heartbeat. ✦

One way my brain will heal, the outpatient psychiatrist tells me, is by sealing over memory, creating a kind of amnesia.

In what way exactly am I spared? ✦

When Sophie is five, she displays the DVD case for *The Story of the Weeping Camel* on the dresser in her bedroom. The film is a narrative documentary about an extended family of nomadic camel herders in the Gobi desert region of Mongolia and their camel, who following a protracted birth in spring rejects her first-born calf. Much of the story is told from the perspective of a younger brother; the warmth of this family stands in contrast to the desolate environment and their semi-permanent residence. In the film, the calf stands alone and cries for its mother. There are repeated failed attempts by family members to reestablish nursing. When the calf rejects bottle feeding, the two young brothers set out across the desert to find a musician who can play a traditional song which, in legend, will cause the pair to reunite. The boys return to their family with word that a violinist is coming; when he arrives and plays his violin, the mother camel weeps and begins to nurse.

I know from Sophie's careful placement of the film in her room that I no longer have to wonder how it is I will explain to her what happened to us. She was there. She already knows. ✦

My father brings me to my first acting audition one year after my parents divorce. We sit in the red velvet seats of the Brookfield Community Playhouse in Connecticut, the town where I live in a house on a lake with my mother, my stepfather, and my sister Roberta. Rehearsing a scene from Lillian Hellman's *The Children's Hour*, a play set in a 1930s girls' boarding school, my father and I practice in the theater amid the chatter of budding teens and wait for my name to be called. Just shy of ten, I'm cast in the part of Rosalie Wells, a timid student who is manipulated into substantiating the accusations of a lesbian affair between the school's headmistresses. A racy storyline even in 1978. Many children my age are not permitted to attend the performance. My challenge is to learn to belt out the line that closes Act I: *I did it, I did it, I did it!* Whether it was true or not, my culpability fills the auditorium. A child of divorce, it's not difficult for me to feel responsible for things. ✦

The same week that I call the Puget Sound Blood Center and my OB, I also call St. Mark's Cathedral in the Capitol Hill neighborhood of Seattle. I want to schedule a baptism. Immediately. I imagine my mother and my stepfather Joe, my mother's first husband Bob—the father of my three older siblings—and my father all in attendance: some sort of synthesis of a fractured family. The woman who answers the phone at St. Mark's informs me that they don't typically perform baptisms on newborn infants. ✦

Driving home from school one day soon after my parents divorce, my mother explains that she is considering moving us to the Canary Islands but is also weighing a relationship with a man she has recently been dating who came for her in a limousine. These are the current contenders for our future.

Instead, she goes to work at Groliers Publishing Company in Connecticut where my sister works and we meet my soon-to-be stepfather Joe at the pool. *He was the only man reading the New York Times!* my mother explains when she tells people about their courtship. ✦

I move to Arizona with my mother and Joe in December of 1980, the year I turn twelve. We make our way cross-country following a travel planner from AAA; we pull our belongings in a U-Haul behind my mother's Lincoln Continental. In our hotel room in Arkansas, I wake to news of John Lennon's assassination. Neil Diamond's "Love on the Rocks" plays again and again.

They rent a two-story stucco unit in a modest neighborhood fronted by a carport and palm trees, across the street from a pool belonging to the development. We swim outside in December. I plaster the walls of my room with a collection of Broadway *Playbills* and photos from my recent community theater production. I try to hold on to both worlds at once.

During the time we live here, I develop a curious reaction to the faucet in my bathroom sink. When I turn on the water, the sound of it suddenly amplifies in a way that I register not just with my ears but also with my gut, an awareness of its shifting volume with no apparent explanation other than there being something in me that hears it differently. I never speak to anyone about this reaction, this sensory experience—the world, specifically the water— suddenly intensified. Perhaps this is because I can still shut it off. And how can one explain exactly? The pain of the water pouring from the faucet, too dangerous to release. ✦

There seems to have been a collective haze and intermittently a shroud surrounding my father's mental illness. *I had no idea going in . . . ,* my mother will say. *When I called your grandmother Dorothy to tell her about the divorce, she said, "Oh dear, and I thought you would be his salvation."* And my mother was his salvation—until eventually she wasn't.

The same might be said in the reverse. ✦

I had the impression from my mother that my father lived in nine-year cycles. His marriage to his first wife Sheila, and to my mother, had each lasted this period of time. When my parents separate the summer before my ninth birthday, I tell my friend Kate that my father isn't going to love me anymore once I turn nine. There is a real possibility I will lose him. ✦

When I call to ask my mother if she remembers her Jackie O. coat, her memory is immediate. *Oh I know exactly what coat I was wearing when I saw Jackie Onassis in the elevator. It was double-breasted with a peter pan collar and brass buttons. Black and white. I can see it in my mind.*

Regarding my father's illness, she is uncertain. *I'm not sure exactly what the diagnosis was but something to do with his personality. After we married, I remember being told that he had schizophrenia.* I remind her that he had what was then called manic depression. *Oh, that's right,* she says.

I used to think that my compulsion to correct my mother, to fact-check, seemed a little cruel, especially when I receive similar shoring up by my own children. Now I realize that it is my best effort to retain her, to keep her with me, to make her real. ✦

My father rarely spoke about his first wife, apart from her name: Sheila. She was more of a fact, a sound. What information I had about her came indirectly, through a kind of intergenerational osmosis. I learned that they had married out of college in the mid-1950s, that she had gone to Bryn Mawr and he to Haverford. But perhaps more importantly to my father, a boy from Ohio, she was a New Yorker and he had set his sights on New York.

On a summer afternoon in 1980, the year I turn twelve, my father takes me shopping at a thrift store in Greenwich Village. Having recently moved with my mother and stepfather to Scottsdale, the mecca of the outdoor mall, I feel hesitant to look through old clothes. My father, on the other hand, a man with an unrelenting appetite for creative ideas, enters the store with the same enthusiasm that he gives to roller blades or the electric car.

Passing by an initial rack of clothing, he turns his attention toward a dress that is carefully pinned to the wall as a display: a bright paisley wrap-around tied at the waist. My father pauses there for a moment and then asks the sales clerk if she can take the dress down for him. I watch from behind as he pulls off his glasses and examines the dress close-up. He holds the back of the neckline, just above the designer tag, and then points to a white label. I lean in over his shoulder to make out the red cursive lettering: *Sheila Katz*.

Oh I'm not paying for this dress, he laughs passing it back to the sales clerk. *I've paid for this dress once already.*

The dress is as close as I ever come to knowing Sheila Katz, so I'm left to imagine her and the day of their dramatic parting. It was her birthday, according to family lore, the summer of 1966. Would she have been turning thirty-four? Thirty-five? I see her wearing a similar *Mad Men* fashion, a sexy Megan Draper affair in reds and oranges with matching lipstick and large hoop earrings. She sets her hair in a Priscilla Presley-esque bouffant, presses her lips on a piece of tissue paper and then heads to the living room to pour herself a celebratory gin and tonic. Now ready at the appointed time, 6 pm, no 6:15 pm, she anticipates my father walking in the door of their apartment on the Upper Westside of Manhattan.

Giving him a few more minutes, she lights a Winston cigarette and then sets it in a nearby ashtray to put on the Beatles album *Revolver*, side two. She sings along with McCartney's "Good Day, Sunshine," but by the time the album reaches "Got to Get You into My Life"—my father's all-time favorite—she has a hunch that something's wrong. I'm not sure how many drinks or how many albums it takes before she registers that he isn't coming. He never does return. He reaches their exit on the Westside Drive and keeps right on going.

I've always thought it unimaginable that a man could leave a woman on her birthday, but my hunch is that he had no more warning than she did. Likely caught in the trajectory of a manic swing, he shed his life like an overcoat, setting it to the side with little thought of its impact. Or perhaps a partner's birthday is a day on which things become *all too real*—the pressure of relationship magnified to meet expectation, tipping the balance of a questionable stability.

There was some rationale: he was living a false life, the life of a business-man—one he would live again with my mother when the weight of family returned—and each time he would abandon his marriage for music, his constant mistress. The overcoat was a gift from his parents, Dorothy and Taylor, who deemed a career in music unacceptable: an oxymoron. In my imagination, there's been no fight, no outward conflict resulting in his disappearance. Sheila is incidental to the problem. She is a casualty. My father will spend his life suiting up and disrobing, never quite comfortable in his own skin. ✦

On the day of my release from the psychiatric unit, I stand next to my trusted nurse at the roundabout, staring at a large desk calendar. I study the date, knowing that this will be a question I'll be asked in what I hope is an exit interview with the psychiatrist on duty. *If you can remember the date,* the nurse coaches me, *and if you could attend just one of the therapy groups, I think the psychiatrist will recommend that you go home this afternoon.* So far, I haven't attended any groups. I'm not even aware that there are groups. Roger had assured me that my only responsibility on the ward was to rest; when the wildness of hallucination reached its peak, I could no longer navigate the world outside the confines of my hospital room. ✦

I manage to get the date right and agree to attend a social skills group with some adolescents on the ward. I wince when I take in the group leader, who I determine is younger than me and performing a job I'm technically licensed to fulfill. I have the thought that I should *pretend* not to have social skills. We sit around a brown laminate table and practice how to invite a friend to a movie. I look at a dark-haired teenaged boy with whom I've watched television before in the patient lounge, by which I mean staring at a television screen. I ask him, *Michael, would you like to go to a movie with me?* It seems to my mind in that moment a completely absurd activity.

And yet, when I return to my room, I sit down at a small desk to draw on a coloring page with markers. I color two tiger goldfish, singing to myself, *Down in the meadow in an itty bitty pool / swam three little fishies and a mama fishy too . . . .* This is a song that my mother and my stepfather Joe would sing. It was part of the repertoire they pulled out at family events and dinner parties. During my stay in the hospital, I hear them singing. They live there in the interstitial space between the walls. ✦

When I look through a box of papers that I've stored away from the period following Sophie's birth, I find the coloring sheet that verifies my memory. It's partially completed. I've colored the body of one fish blue with red scales. A second fish, behind the first, has the beginnings of markings in red in what looks to be a plan for a contrasting color scheme.

It's difficult for me to acknowledge that I was a thirty-year-old new mother coloring in a child's coloring book. Pretending that I didn't have social skills. Missing my baby and my husband. Wanting to go home.

That said, coloring is said to be akin to meditation. An expressive therapy encouraging grounding.

Included in a box of materials I've saved from the period of my psychosis is the Overlake Hospital Team B Schedule. I guess that makes me a Team B alum. A typical Monday includes:

7:00 am	Grooming
8:00–8:30 am	Breakfast and Meds
9:45–10:30 am	Exercise Group
11:00–11:30 am	Discharge Group
11:45–12:15 pm	Lunch and Meds
12:30–1:00 pm	Focus Group (crafts or games)
3:45–4:15 pm	Goals Group
5:00–5:15 pm	Stretching
5:30–5:45 pm	Dinner and Meds
6:30–7:00 pm	Focus Group
9:00 pm	Meds
10:30 pm	Bed by 11 pm

I read: *Treatment on this unit is based mainly on group therapy and milieu involvement.* I seem to have been an anomaly. I don't recall seeing any other mothers and babies on the ward.

My admission papers from the ER indicate that I'm being treated for insomnia requiring a medication evaluation and for depression and anxiety. I'm referred for group treatment to improve coping skills. This is not yet the correct diagnosis. ✦

From time to time growing up, my mother tells me that she has had experiences of seeing things before they happen. She tells me about the night that her father died unexpectedly of cardiac arrest in a chair in his living room in Seattle. *Your father and I were at a dinner party in Connecticut when I suddenly felt my dad's presence as if he had come to say goodbye. I told your father that something was wrong and we had to excuse ourselves from the party. When we walked through the door of our house, the phone was already ringing. It was my sister calling to tell me that Daddy had died.* ✦

My mom gave me ESP and she's the only one who can take it back. I've written this on a sheet of graph paper during my time on the psychiatric ward. ✦

I'm scared of everything now, I've written on a notebook page. *Tell me that you think it's the ESP that needs to be undone.* The page is a conversation with the staff member assigned to my room at night. We must be writing in an effort to be quiet. ✦

The process of writing this story reminds me of an episode from *Homeland* where Carrie Mathison, a CIA agent with a history of bipolar disorder, attempts to prove that a senior Marine held in captivity has been flipped by Al-Qaeda and is planning a terrorist attack on American soil. Obsessed with her suspect, Mathison is found frantically trying to connect data points: photos and notes posted on a wall size whiteboard at her home. She has drawn arrows in red attempting to indicate the relationships between what admittedly looks like scrawl. Mathison works tirelessly to connect the fragments and, while initially hospitalized and dismissed from service for the CIA, if you watch enough episodes, her theory proves right. ✦

And there is the understandable fear that I will be left sitting here on the floor of my office, a madwoman surrounded by scraps of paper, my piles of fragments, unable to find a through line. ✦

Just two months before my younger daughter Camille's birth, an intuitive healer on an island in British Columbia retrospectively explains my postpartum psychosis as a fractured aura: an inversion of psychic skin. *You were thrust into seeing unprepared,* she says.

Does this qualify me as a witch?

A psychic gift that needs to be trained through gradual integration. Birth as possible initiation rite. These are the notes I have written in a spiral notebook covered in a pattern of green Celtic knots.

I google Celtic knots and read: *The basic four-cord knot looks like three strands of hair braided.*

The spiral in ancient Celtic culture represented the sun. A double spiral represented the equinox—a time of year when the length of day and night are equal. In other cultures, two spirals represent the yin and yang.

This is my riff on insanity: endless association. ✦

For several months after returning home from the psychiatric hospital, I can't close my eyes without seeing visuals. A perpetual black and white film of garbled imagery plays on a continuous loop: menacing faces, the shadows of fuchsia plants. I seem to remember that I should only see darkness, but I have to confirm this with Roger. *What do you see when you close your eyes?* I ask him.

Were I to be a witch, I would like to be an oracle.

Psychotic symptoms: the *unaspirated voices* of our ancestors, one analytic paper suggests. ✦

Parental narcissism. Intergenerational patterns of interaction impacting personality and biochemistry. The intuitive healer, these are the letters that come after her name: Ph.D., RCC, ATR, RPT-S, CPT-S. She is a trauma specialist who teaches internationally on expressive play therapy for children. She was my teacher and now my consultant.

Also noted: *Roger and I suffered simultaneous trauma.* I don't know that I've said this enough.

Roger suffered a trauma.

In the intuitive's studio in British Columbia, a photograph of a patch of snow in the garden with the imprint of a rose. The energetic residue of a rose: its aura. ✦

296.04
Bipolar 1 D/O
Single manic episode
With severe psychotic features
Postpartum onset ✦

Pupils dilated, 5mm bilaterally and reactive. ✦

FAMILY PSYCHIATRIC HISTORY: Notable for father with bipolar mood disorder. ✦

May all beings be free from suffering. A prayer of loving-kindness. ✦

One year after my hospitalization, I'm invited to sit on the board of directors of an organization that supports the prevention and treatment of postpartum mood disorders. I realize in accepting this invitation that I may have contact with the nurse practitioner who had mistaken my mania for postpartum depression. She offers to meet with me at her office, which looks unfamiliar despite my having been there several times before. She brings me a copy of a recently published book on hormones and women's moods. The dust jacket is purple and the book rests on a table in the area where we stand between two chairs. *I guess I didn't want it to be the case*, she says, handing me her humanity, *my mother had bipolar disorder following my birth.* ✦

You might want to consider, Roger counsels me in the weeks after my hospitalization, *the impact of disclosure.* For quite awhile, I assume that disclosure is a given. I believe that people can tell I've been crazy the moment they look at me, as if I have a large poster on my head: *recently psychotic,* and so announcing that I've had a postpartum mood disorder will merely break the ice.

For a time, I fear that I can no longer be a therapist. ✦

There is a nurse on the ward whose name is Venus. I call her Mars. I can't tell you why I privilege one planet over another, only that she makes a lasting impression. She is the first to take me outside, invite me to take my shoes off, place my bare feet in the grass.

This will make you better at what you do, she says rubbing her brown toes against the earth. ✦

Would you mind sitting in the hallway? I've only just realized that the young female nurse assigned to my room is a separate being from me. This is the day I turn the corner. ✦

Repeat internally, *"I am enough,"* my yoga teacher says with gentle conviction. ✦

A few weeks after I return from the psychiatric unit, my sister Roberta carries two-month-old Sophie into my room just as I'm going to sleep. Roberta is on the current rotation of family members and doulas caring for me in the wake of my illness. Gripping hold of my sanity, I cling to my psychiatrist's recommendations, including sleeping separately from Sophie in order to preserve my sleep. Later I will learn that Sophie also prefers her space when sleeping, but for the time being I experience our separation as a perpetual loss.

What kind of mother can't hear her baby in the night? I ask Roger on more than one occasion. He strokes my hair. I berate myself this way until I learn that not hearing her is a residual, and temporary, effect of medication.

For now, I struggle to believe that sleep is even within my power. I'm governed by routine. At 8 pm, I nurse Sophie; afterwards I take my prescription, minimizing her exposure. I drink milk that Roger has warmed on the stove from a green ceramic mug. I take a bath. I remind myself that I've slept the night before. I place my legs up the wall behind my bed, set my head on a pillow, and breathe for quite awhile. I do this each night—in the same order—but each time it seems as if I'm starting over and the length of each segment grows. One night, Roger asks me if my bedtime routine might in fact be keeping me from sleeping. I'm not yet able to consider this possibility.

When Roberta enters the room with Sophie, who is swaddled in a pale blue sleeper fastened at the bottom with tiny white buttons, it's as if she's delivering a present. How exciting to see Sophie, to nuzzle her in my room as during her first few weeks of life. My sister leaves us together. I trust she will return. And while I fear that I'm breaking a rule, I also realize that something is being returned to me. I'm once again a mother who can hold her baby in bed.

It's a quiet summer evening, warm, and the windows are open beneath the shades. I hold Sophie against my chest, our faces pointed toward each other, our cheeks touching. I can feel her rib cage expand and contract with her breath. I hear each little baby noise. And then I feel her nose, brushing back and forth against mine in the dark. She does this for quite some time, long enough for me to be certain that it's happening.

I will tell Sophie this memory more times than are necessary. ✦

When Sophie's nose brushes against mine, *I am enough.* ✦

Sometime during my ninth month of pregnancy with Camille in August of 2003, I walk into the grocery store in our neighborhood to pick up some milk. As I head past the bakery and smoothie stand at the entry, the world suddenly grows very loud, the volume turned way up. I press my hands against my ears but I can't shut out the chatter of conversation in the café. The room is a house of mirrors: faces distorted convex and concave, an exaggerated cheekbone, the bridge of a nose, a body caving in on itself at the stomach. And all along the unending chatter. I watch from behind what seems like a thin layer of cellophane and I'm nauseated by the smell of coffee beans.

Now I'm dodging the assault of fluorescent lighting. How I feel is afraid. So I push myself past the scream of sensation and out the nearest exit. Just this act is a triumph.

I try to talk myself down as I walk along the urban street toward our house. I attempt what my psychiatrist refers to as thought stopping. *That's enough for today. I'll think about you again tomorrow.* I actually repeat these words out loud as I'm walking. *That's enough for today. I'll think about you again tomorrow.* I always assumed this kind of therapeutic advice was useless until I was desperate. So on my walk, I breathe and try to thought stop, but the noise of cars on the busy urban street is impossible to shut out. It's undeniably loud and I'm a woman on the verge of childbirth with its associated heightened sensitivity to sound.

Once in the house, alone, I retreat to the front bedroom that Roger and I share with its sage green walls and view of a large red Japanese Maple. I curl up against a long down pillow, wrapping my arms and legs against its soft mass, and try to convince myself that this is not the illness descending. Wiping. Out. My. Brain. Taking me away. *Light of the divine spirit world envelop me.* ✦

In the hospital room where I birth Camille primarily in water, I create an altar: a dark purple scarf lined with fringe spread over a table; photographs of Sophie, now four-and-a-half-years old, one with a white daisy stuck in her braid standing on a roadside on an island in British Columbia, another playing with Roger in a sprinkler in our backyard in Seattle; four mandala print coasters; an avocado-shaped candle; and lavender.

I wear a silver Navajo necklace with turquoise and coral stones, an amulet purchased on a trip to Scottsdale to visit my mother and Joe and, for a time, a blue shawl knit by a group of women at a church outside of Boston. Our birth doula Sandy accompanies Roger and me primarily in silence though there is a moment before I enter the water at 2:50 am when I say to her *I'm not sure I can do this, Sandy,* and she responds, *You have all the resource that you need.* At 5 am, I exit the water, go to the bathroom and then get into the bed in a side-lying position with Roger standing close to me. At 5:15 am, the midwife confirms that I am fully dilated and, after 37 minutes of concentrated pushing, Camille is born. The midwife places her on my chest and Roger and I kiss her and hold her fingers. When she has nursed for the first time, Camille sleeps in an adjoining room with our postpartum doula Mary Ellen, who brings Camille to me for feedings, and no one enters the birthing suite, not even for vitals or to clean the floor, unless I've had one full REM cycle of sleep. This is how carefully we are held. For the first six weeks of Camille's life, we wrap ourselves in doula care. *May all beings be free from suffering.* ✦

During the afternoon of the day that Camille is born, September 13, 2003, Sophie comes to the hospital together with my mother and Joe who have been caring for her at home. I can tell from the deliberate but uneven part in Sophie's hair that my mother has helped her to braid it. They arrive with the thrill of new grandparents and the quiet skepticism of an older sister. Sophie opens a package that turns out to be a pair of pink leather ballet slippers given as a gift from Camille. And while she's not buying it, she holds her back straight as she cradles Camille in her arms, propped up by a group of pillows and, when this grows tiring, she heads off to an adjoining courtyard with Roger to play on a large metal slide. ✦

In July of 2008, the year that Sophie turned nine, I set about telling the stories of other women with postpartum mood disorders. I spend a day interviewing Jane Honikman, founder of Postpartum Support International, at her home in Southern California. She shows me a large collection of newspaper articles and letters beginning in the early 1970s, including one sent to Gloria Steinem. *When one door was closed to me,* Honikman says over lunch at her kitchen table, *I'd simply knock on another.* Jane championed a consumer-based movement to support women with postpartum depression and to demand its recognition by the health care system. Eventually, the American Psychological Association would add the qualifier under Mood Disorders: with *postpartum onset* to its Diagnostic and Statistical Manual of Mental Disorders.

Steinem cautioned against further medicalizing women's birth experiences. To my mind, they both had a point.

In the fall of the same year, I meet with Michelle Oberman, a friend and legal scholar. While she responds to my questions about the incarceration of women for crimes committed during a postpartum psychosis, in the end she encourages me to turn the lens back to myself. ✦

A recording of Sophie's response to a section of this writing, age 15:

The cords that keep you connected to others, you can also get entangled in or trapped. The length of each section seemed like it was interesting, your choices, because of how they'd be coming back to you bit by bit or how difficult they were for you to recall. It could have something to do with the length or the depth of them.

You know when you're reading "The Catcher in the Rye" and every time Holden talks about something important for him, or traumatic for him, or hard for him to talk about, he stops talking about himself and starts talking about you. He has to pull himself away from how difficult it is for him. Kind of like that. ✦

While proximity to memory is difficult, it's true, so are gaps in memory. One reason I fear not being able to remember the period of my illness is because I equate the absence of memory with my absence from Sophie. The very thing I did not want to be.

Even when Sarah was totally unreachable, she would smile when she saw her daughter.

I move into the not remembering, the silence, the space, the inarticulable.

My therapist reminds me that we each have psychotic elements in the mind, psychotic with a small p and not a capital P. ✦

Traumatic memory, I read, is insufficiently encoded; it is a memory *shot through with holes.*

When I read this, I imagine myself looking down the long barrel of a rifle, my cheek pressed toward the stock, my eyes set to the scope. With the pressure of my fingers at the trigger, I feel the piercing force of the gun firing, the recoil.

In the writing of these pages, I am at once the target and the shot.

Each hole a little wound. Each hole a new opening. The opening of tight spaces. ✦

In August of 2013, my stepfather Joe is diagnosed with colon cancer. He is 88 years old at the time of his diagnosis, still playing doubles tennis in the heat of the Scottsdale summer and driving his Buick. He and my mother have happy hour around a glass coffee table with Japanese laquered coasters and she makes him coffee in the morning with Sweet 'N Low. Otherwise, he prefers to do the cooking. It's a tribute to his living that we are surprised that he is dying. When he receives his diagnosis, I'm reminded that we're all dying. What is unusual is that someone is holding a sign in front of his face: *You're dying. Most likely within six months.*

De muerte que no manqué. Joe, a Sephardic Jew whose parents emigrated from Greece, repeats these Ladino words each time we sit down to dinner as an extended family. *De muerte que no manqué,* he repeats and then fills in the name of whichever family member is missing from our table. *De muerte que no manqué: they should not be missing from this table because of death,* he explains. And, as he is always in favor of a good debate, at other times he says just the opposite, *the only reason you should be missing from this table is because of death.* At his funeral, the Rabbi corrects him. *Death should not be what separates us,* she says.

The following spring, I spend an afternoon in our aging Toyota Tacoma truck so that I can listen to a cassette recording of my father rehearsing a nightclub cabaret toward the end of his life. Our truck is old school, having clocked well over 200,000 miles, and has windows that roll down, a stick shift and, most importantly, a cassette player. While I could sing each of the songs on the tape from memory, I'm amused to discover that the music my father arranged with a consistent jazzy flare in fact has tremendous range: anything from Noel Coward to the Pointer Sisters, but always love songs.

It occurs to me as I transcribe the lyrics and patter from the tape that in fact I'm creating a medley, an overture of sorts. I recognize in that moment that I have two fathers and that one of them is dying in the present while I'm eulogizing the one who has already passed.

I forward the cassette tape first with my finger and then by inserting and twisting a pencil. This is the recommended method I learn when I read the now-yellowed insert from the case. I push open the tape deck and blow into its opening. The cassette player is making a disconcerting clicking sound and has stopped responding to the rewind and forward buttons. Each time I fiddle with it, I wonder if the tape will break and if it's the last time that I will hear my father's voice.

When caring for Joe over nine days in a hospice facility, I learn how to love someone in the midst of losing them. I'm learning to be in relationship to things that are dying. *De muerte que no manqué.* Death should not be what separates us.

My mother is in the habit of saying that she and Joe had seven children. They were in agreement on this. In fact, they had a total of seven children between them from three separate marriages. This reality seems too painful for my mother to bear.

Only in accompanying him through his death did I begin to acknowledge that my stepfather had in fact been a father to me. This truth seems less threatening to me now. ✦

If you see the spine as luminous with the flicking of the wind against the pen you use to write the body, would this be satisfactory? I write this question to myself in a notebook during a seminar on hybrid writing with the poet and trauma writer Bhanu Kapil. And I recall, as a way of remembering, the intuitive healer encouraging me on the telephone from her office in British Columbia to imagine the light around me as a blue egg. *Light of the divine spirit world envelop me.* These are the words I was instructed to repeat, and then she said, *I don't want to take you away from where you are.* She said, *I will leave you now.* Or was it *I want to return you to yourself now, so that I don't take you away from where you are.* She soothed me with this wording and the blue light, or better yet, the idea that I was held within it. ✦

More than hormones, I now think in terms of holding environments. ✦

When my yoga teacher asks if anyone is cold and needs a blanket during our ending Shavasana, the pose where we practice death, I feel pressure in my throat and then tears. I see the face of the psychoanalyst Margaret Little in my mind whose book *Psychotic Anxieties and Containment* I'd read the night before. I had studied her photo on the dust jacket as I made my way through the pages of her account of an analysis with the pediatrician Donald Winnicott, who *through many long hours held my two hands clasped between his, almost like an umbilical cord, while I lay, often hidden beneath the blanket. Silent, inert, withdrawn, in panic, rage, or tears asleep and sometimes dreaming . . . . It was as if I needed to take into myself the silence and stillness that he provided.*

I feel as if I am crying both *for* and *to* Margaret Little. I think of my mother as a child in her breathing tent and want to reach out to that vulnerable little girl. ✦

I've learned that my body is the one who remembers. Memory is lodged there in fragmented pieces regurgitated or coughed up in moments of unpredicted release. At times, I feel inhabited or perhaps overtaken.

Exiting the ferry terminal on the commuter boat that crosses Puget Sound from Bainbridge Island to Seattle some months ago, I walk in step with the other commuters, my Frye cowboy boots keeping pace with the leather business shoes of attorneys and bankers headed with briefcases and umbrellas toward their downtown office buildings. As I disembark, the trigger not apparent to me, tears stream down my face and I close my eyes and press my lips together, not breathing for a moment and then taking a series of short deep inhalations. A man in a pressed white shirt approaches and asks if he might help me find my way. I brush my hair back from my face, pull on the zipper of my down jacket at the collar, and assure him, still walking, that I'm really okay. No longer fighting the deluge of emotion, I make my way past Pike Place Market toward my therapist's office, a route I've walked enough times to wear grooves in the sidewalk. I go on like this for several blocks, at times noticing the lingering glance of another concerned passerby, a woman in a blue gray trench coat, then a man with dreadlocks and a beaded necklace, but I'm freed in a way by my inability to hold back the convulsions. I walk another block, maybe two, past a floral shop and Le Pichet bistro and then I find myself sitting on the ledge of a planter next to a homeless man, his eyes, glazed but kind, staring forward toward the street. In that moment, I feel like my being extends beyond my body, our proximity a comfort. I feel as if I *am* him. ✦

There is a yoga sutra that says that God is the part of you that is unchanging. The question is how to be in relationship with things that are dying, to live in the face of loss. ✦

As I collect these various fragments, even without full assemblage, I am overtaken by sorrow that my father died still unadhered, fragmented by his illness. And as for my desire to ease his suffering, it has taken me this long to gather up the pieces.

Still, this portrait of a madman, I can sit with it now.

In a recent dream, I hold a piece of fabric: a broad weave with rows of uneven circular holes, porous, made of flesh. Pulling it taut between my hands, I sense its integrity. ✦

Fetal cells cross the placenta during pregnancy and provide benefits to the mother's health throughout her lifetime. *Mother and child are linked at the cellular level,* one article says.

When I think of history through this lens, one which conceives our existence as moving in multiple directions simultaneously, influencing the generations which precede us and those that come after, I start for the first time to experience what I believe to be a variant on what the German philosopher Friedrich Nietzsche describes as the *eternal recurrence* of time. ✦

Last night, Roger pressed against my body as if he knew the exact location of its pain. With significant pressure, he ran the tips of his fingers down my neck and throat, pressing deeply against the skin, alongside my rib cage, across my intercostal muscles and into my lower left pelvis. An offering. A moment of grace. He was making love to me through the spiral that is my body. ✦

Camille, now twelve, is studying astronomy with her sixth grade class and tells me that the cosmos is a spiral. It appears that *we live in a spiral galaxy called the Milky Way in a minor arm of a multi-galaxy spiraling universe.*

Not to mention that the spiral helix is the shape of our DNA.

Our sun, formed more than 4 billion years ago, has traveled around the galaxy sixteen times. The universe moves more slowly than our individual lifespan, more slowly than the collective memory of multiple generations.

Soon after learning this, I dream about a pencil with a metal compass: spinning. ✦

(2013–2016)

Acknowledgments

Immense gratitude to Colleen O'Connor and Abigail Zimmer for the sensitivity and precision of your editorial responses. Thank you to Ryan Spooner for designing such beautiful covers for books published by The Lettered Streets Press.

Endless appreciation to the faculty and staff of the Creative Writing program at Goddard College, especially Beatrix Gates, Victoria Nelson, Bhanu Kapil, and Aimee Liu. Thank you to Michelle Saunders and Tina Cachules for inspiring me to enroll.

Special thanks to Kim Townsend, Judy K. Eekhoff, Penny Simkin, Austin Case, Joan Fiset, Brant Pope, and Natalie Singer for reading drafts of this book; and to Jane Honikman, Michelle Shellenberger, Shana Turner, Angelisa Russo, Dana Watkins Montanari, Katrina Barnes, Theresa Barker, Jeff Steele, Mike Fosmark, and Cindy Heidelberg for your guidance regarding specific fragments.

I am forever grateful for your encouragement, Claire Dederer. If feminist were a verb, that's what you've done for me.

Thank you, Theo Pauline Nestor, for helping me to find my voice and for your perpetual advocacy.

Gratitude to my yoga teachers who facilitated the writing of this book.

Thank you to my former neighbors at PBV who cheered me on as I walked to and from my office!

Thank you to my first writing partners, Sonja Fritts and Ellie Linen Low.

Thanks and love to the Lovelies for holding space as a community of writers, and to "my poet" Laura Schaeffer for exchanging new writing with me. Thank you to Penny Hinke for your company and humor, to Sarah Cannon and Lynn Keating Smith for your consistent support, to Liz Kellebrew for alerting me to submissions, and to Storm Blue whose spoken word inspired me.

Thank you to my father, Peter, for imparting a love of the arts.

It should be noted that psychoanalysis is a collaborative conversation and, in that sense, this book is coauthored.

Deep appreciation for all who cared for me during my pregnancies and following the birth of my two daughters.

Love and gratitude to my mother, Myrna, for bringing me into the world, and to Roger, Sophie, and Camille for making my life whole.

Sarah C. Townsend is the author of *Setting the Wire: A Memoir of Postpartum Psychosis* (Lettered Streets Press, 2019). Her essays have appeared in *The Writer in the World* and *Pitkin Review*, and a coauthored paper with Elisabeth Young-Bruehl serves as a chapter in *Subject to Biography: Pschoanalysis, Feminism and Writing Women's Lives*. Sarah received her MFA in creative writing from Goddard College, her master's in counseling psychology from Northwestern University, and is a graduate of the College of Letters at Wesleyan University. She writes, teaches, and practices psychotherapy in Seattle, WA. You can learn more about her at SarahCTownsend.com.

Other Books by Lettered Streets Press

Supper & Repair Kit by Nicole Wilson (2014)

Regret by Ryan Spooner (2014)

The Blank Target by Robert Alan Wendeborn (2015)

Way Elsewhere by Julie Trimingham (2016)

Louise & Louise & Louise by Olivia Cronk (2016)

The Way I've Seen Her Ever Since by David Bersell (2017)

Starfish by Sara Goodman (2018)

Split Series

Vol. I (2014)
This Will Be His Legacy by Aubrey Hirsch
Bone Matter by Alexis Pope

Vol. II (2015)
Birds As Leaves by Melanie Sweeney
Seven Sunsets by Jasmine Dreame Wagner

Vol. III (2016)
The Most Dangerous Game by Megan Giddings
The Romances by Lo Kwa Mei-en

www.letteredstreetspress.com